W9-BDL-754

Everything You Need to Know About

STAYING
SAFE IN
CYBERSPACE

The Internet can be an incredible tool for getting information.

• THE NEED TO KNOW LIBRARY •

Everything You Need to Know About

STAYING SAFE IN CYBERSPACE

Jennifer Croft

1999

THE ROSEN PUBLISHING GROUP, INC.
NEW YORK

Published in 1999 by The Rosen Publishing Group, Inc.
29 East 21st Street, New York, NY 10010

First Edition

Library of Congress Cataloging-in-Publication Data

Croft, Jennifer, 1970–
    Everything you need to know about staying safe in cyberspace/ by Jennifer Croft.
        p.   cm. — (The need to know library)
    Includes bibliographical references and index.
    Summary: Examines some of the dangers that might be encountered while using the Internet, and gives advice about how to avoid them.
    ISBN 0-8239-2957-4
    1. Internet (Computer network) and children—United States Juvenile literature. 2. Computer crimes—United States—Prevention Juvenile literature. [1. Internet (Computer network)—Safety measures. 2. Safety.] I. Title. II. Series.
HQ784.I58C76   1999
303.48'33'083—dc21   99-16887
                                                                    CIP

Manufactured in the United States of America

Contents

Introduction

Miranda could not wait to get home from school. Her best friend, Wen, had asked if she wanted to go to the mall, but Miranda said no. "I've got too much homework," she said as she hurried out the door of the classroom.

But Miranda wasn't really going home to do homework—she was going home to check her e-mail. Every day for the past month, she had been exchanging messages with a guy named Toby, who lived in another city. They had "met" in a chat room and had been writing one another ever since.

It seemed to Miranda that she and Toby had a lot in common. She felt comfortable telling him all about her problems and feelings even though they had never met face-to-face. Sometimes she felt closer to Toby than she felt to Wen. That's why she hadn't even told Wen—or anybody else—about Toby.

Miranda was starting to feel as though she and Toby really connected, and Toby wrote that he felt the same way. In a message he sent a few days ago, Toby had asked Miranda for her telephone number, but Miranda said that she would have to think about it. She had heard stories about bad things happening to people who met through e-mail—but she had also heard about people who met the person of their dreams that way. She wanted to be adventurous, but she didn't want to get into trouble.

The Internet is one of the greatest inventions of the twentieth century. It provides an easy way for people to communicate, get information, and conduct business. Using the Internet may not be a big deal to you, but remember that it was not a part of your grandparents' or even your parents' lives when they were growing up. In fact, the Internet has only become a part of ordinary life in the last five years or so. It has grown amazingly quickly in ways that nobody expected. It will probably change and grow even more in your lifetime.

While the Internet is an incredible tool, it is also something with which you should be careful. The fact that the Internet is accessible to anyone, anywhere, at any time is what makes it so fantastic—but that is also what gives it the potential for danger.

The dangers of the Internet are real. In 1997, the FBI increased its staff devoted to computer crimes by 50 percent to address the growing problem of computer-related

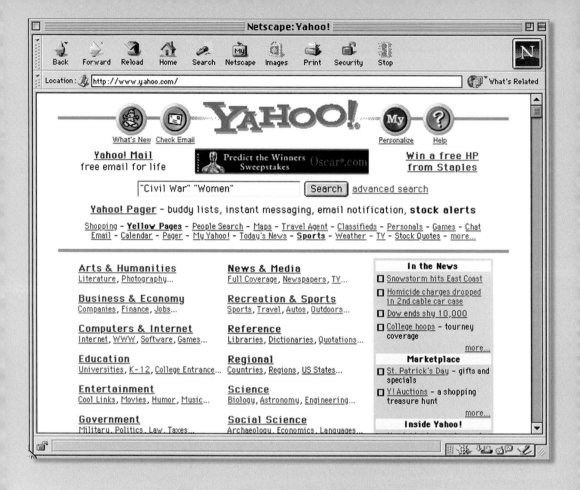

This is just one of the many types of search screens.

exploitation of children and teenagers. You have the right to be protected from harassment, abusive treatment, and discrimination—both on-line and off.

An event that captured headlines in the nation's newspapers in 1998 alerted many people to the potential dangers of cyberspace. In the spring of that year, Oliver Jovanovic, a thirty-one-year-old graduate student at Columbia University in New York City, was convicted of kidnapping and sexually abusing a young female college student whom he had "met" in an Internet chat room. He was sentenced to fifteen years in prison.

Jovanovic and the young woman had been carrying on a regular e-mail correspondence; one day, she agreed to go to dinner with him. After dinner, she went to Jovanovic's apartment, where he committed the crimes for which he was convicted.

Like many people in similar circumstances, the victim in the Jovanovic case believed that because she had exchanged a number of e-mail messages with Jovanovic, he was no longer a stranger. However, it is important to remember that someone you "know" just from the Internet *is* a stranger. Therefore, you need to exercise the same kind of caution with people you meet on the Net that you would with any other stranger.

Playing It Safe

This book will explain the basic concepts of the Internet, including descriptions of some of the ways that you might use the Net. It will warn you of some of the dangers you may encounter while using the Internet and will give you advice on avoiding these dangers. After reading this book, we hope that you will be able to use the power of the Internet to your advantage while also keeping yourself safe.

Oliver Jovanovic was convicted of sexually abusing a woman with whom he had developed an on-line relationship.

Chapter 1

Welcome to the Internet

What is the Internet? The Internet is a global system of computers connected by a huge network. The Internet allows users to communicate with one another and enables the transfer of data or information from one computer to any other computer on the same network.

To log on to the Internet, you will need a computer with the proper software, a modem (which is often built right into the computer), and a telephone connection. You will also need an Internet Service Provider (ISP) to provide access to the Internet. In some cases, your school may provide Internet access.

Cyberspace

When we talk about "cyberspace," we mean the world that the Internet makes available—a world of individuals,

schools, businesses, libraries, museums, governments, and
many other kinds of people and places that have put information on the Internet. This information is posted on what
is called a Web site.

The term "cyberspace" first appeared in a novel,
Neuromancer, by William Gibson, published in 1984.
Ten years later, in 1994, faster modem connections
became available and the Internet really took off.

The World Wide Web

The Internet is not the same as the World Wide Web. The
World Wide Web was created in 1990 when Tim Berners-
Lee, a researcher at a physics lab in Switzerland, devel-
oped something called HyperText Markup Language
(HTML). At first, scientists thought that the World Wide
Web would be used mainly as a way to distribute scien-
tific information.

The Web works through the hypertext system by allowing users to access text, graphics, illustrations, sound, or
video by means of hypertext links, or hyperlinks. When
people talk about "surfing the Web," they are describing
the act of moving from one hyperlink to another.
Hyperlinks allow you to move from site to site without
needing to know the specific addresses of the sites.

The Web has become the most famous and popular
item on the Internet. To access the Web, you need an
Internet account and software known as a World Wide
Web browser or client. (Netscape, Internet Explorer, and
Mosaic are a few examples of such browsers.)

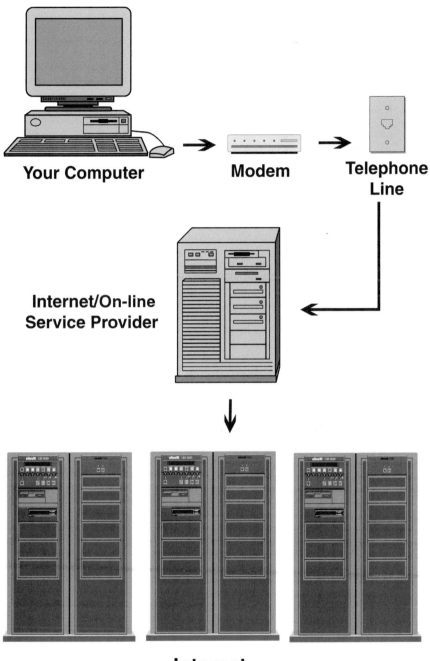

Your Computer **Modem** **Telephone Line**

Internet/On-line Service Provider

Internet

The Internet unites individual computer users through a global network system.

```
┌──────────────────── Welcome to my web site.html ────────────────────┐
│ L·8·· · I · · · I · · · I · · · 2 · · · I · · · 3 · · · I · · · 4 · · · I · · · 5 · · · I · · · 6 · · · I · ▲ · · ▲ │
│  <HTML>¶                                                              │
│  <HEAD>¶                                                              │
│  <META HTTP-EQUIV="Content-Type" CONTENT="text/html; charset=windows-1252">¶ │
│  <META NAME="Generator" CONTENT="Microsoft Word 97/98">¶             │
│  <TITLE>Welcome to my web site</TITLE>¶                              │
│  <META NAME="Template" CONTENT="Mac Attack:Applications:Microsoft Office │
│  98:Templates:Web Pages:Blank Web Page">¶                           │
│  </HEAD>¶                                                             │
│  <BODY LINK="#0000ff" VLINK="#800080">¶                             │
│  ¶                                                                    │
│  <P>Welcome to my web site</P>¶                                      │
│  <P>My likes</P>¶                                                    │
│  ¶                                                                    │
│  <UL>¶                                                                │
│  <LI>Rainy Days</LI>¶                                                 │
│  <LI>Summer</LI>¶                                                     │
│  <LI>Going to the Beach</LI>¶                                         │
│  <LI>Playing the piano</LI></UL>¶                                    │
│  </BODY>¶                                                             │
│  </HTML>¶                                                             │
└──────────────────────────────────────────────────────────────────────┘
```

This is an example of the HTML language.

Who's Using the Internet?

Access to the Internet is increasing all the time in
every corner of the world. According to a recent survey, there are approximately 50 million Internet
users worldwide, 1 million Web sites, and 100 million
Web pages. In the United States alone, more than 36
million people are on-line. Almost half of all
American households have PCs (personal computers). Many companies and organizations have their
own Web sites and use the Internet for many kinds
of business. It has been projected that by 2002 there
will be more than 64 million Internet users just in the
United States.

In 1992, less than 5 million people in America—

approximately 2 percent of the population—used e-mail. Today that number has climbed above 40 million. It has been estimated that in a few years, the number will be 135 million. There are plans under way for the federal government to make e-mail available to the public through terminals at post offices, for example.

Using the Internet at School

More and more schools are going on-line. Some even have their own Web sites. Teachers are using the Internet in the classroom as a teaching and research tool. Even President Bill Clinton has spoken of getting every classroom in America onto the Internet. We may not have quite reached that point yet, but it is probably not far away.

If your school already has access to the Internet, it probably also has an Acceptable Use Policy (AUP). Find out what your school's AUP is and make sure that you are familiar with it. Violating the AUP may result in the loss of your access to the Net at school. Some schools use blocking or filtering software to prevent students from accessing inappropriate sites. Your parents may be asked to sign an agreement with the school about your use of the Internet.

Know *your* rights, too—even if you are accessing the Internet and using e-mail through your school district, you still have the right to free speech under the U.S. Constitution.

More schools provide students with Internet access every day.

Cybershopping

Shopping on the Internet—also known as e-commerce—is increasingly popular. Eighteen percent of people who use the Internet also make purchases on-line. Click a few buttons, type in a credit card number, and anything from a book to an airline ticket can be yours.

What are people buying on the Internet? According to a recent survey, the most common purchases are computer software and hardware. Books are another popular item with cybershoppers. Food, clothing, compact discs, flowers, and even cars are also purchased via the Internet.

There is a lot of cool stuff to buy on the Net, but it is generally better to browse than to buy. While new technology is making on-line credit card purchases safer than ever before, that does not mean that e-commerce is 100 percent safe.

If you want to try cybershopping, go exploring on-line with your parents. Let them make the final decision on whether to buy or not. Even if your parents sometimes let you use their credit cards, don't ever type in their credit card number on-line—always let them make this kind of purchase themselves. After all, they will find out what you bought when they get the credit card bill anyway. It's better to be safe and get their approval up front than to have to explain that bill for ten CDs!

What Else Is On-Line?

As you probably already know, there are Web sites out there for just about every subject imaginable. You may have

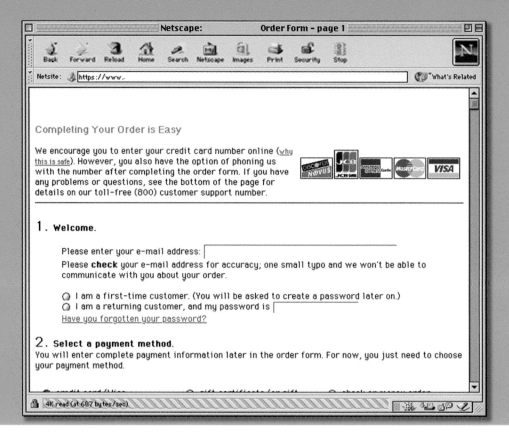

Cybershopping can be tempting.

already used the Web to check out information on your favorite bands, movies, television shows, sports teams, or other hobbies and interests. This is a fun and safe way to explore your interests and learn about things going on all around the world.

There are many sites especially for teens, that provide information on topics of special interest to young people. There are even sites that can help you with your homework! They do not give you any answers, of course, but they make it easy to get information you would otherwise have to look up in an enyclopedia or other reference book.

Chapter 2

Safe Surfing

When is surfing not safe? Along with all of the great and fascinating stuff on the Internet, there is also stuff that is not so great—stuff that is offensive, threatening, or even obscene.

Sometimes sites ask that you "register" at the site. Often this means that you are asked to provide information about yourself before you can fully access the site. Do not register on a site without talking to your parents about it first. Keep in mind that any information you provide will probably be put into a database and used for marketing purposes.

"Cookies" are a technology that make it possible for your "hits" on specific Web pages to be tracked. With user information obtained from cookies, marketing companies change the advertisements or content of a site to match what they think are the interests of the site's users. While

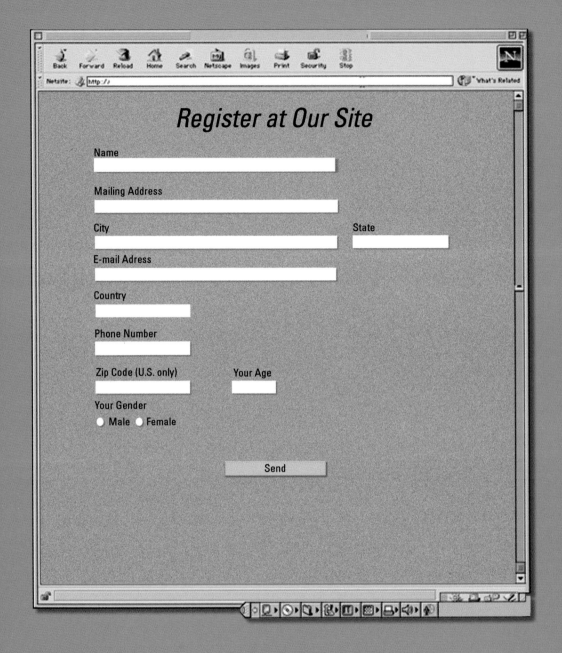

Example of a Web site where the user needs to register.

cookies are not really unsafe, they are invasive. They are another method that companies use to gain information about you and what you might be interested in buying.

The Internet and Your Parents

One day, when Heather's dad went on-line right after Heather logged off, he was able to see what sites she had been visiting. One was a site for a television show that she was not allowed to watch.

Heather was furious when her parents told her that she was not allowed to surf the Web anymore. "You know you shouldn't have visited that site," her dad said. "But since you're so upset, maybe we need to talk more about using the Internet."

That night Heather's family had a meeting to talk about using the Net. Heather said she was upset because she felt as though she was not free to do what she wanted. She also complained that she did not really know what the rules were—she just felt as if she was always breaking them. Heather's parents admitted that they did not really know what the rules were either. They confessed that they did not know as much as they should about the Internet and were worried that there were too many things on-line that would be offensive or harmful to Heather and her brother Michael.

"We don't really know how to keep you from seeing bad things on the Internet," Heather's mom said. "So sometimes it's easier for us to just tell you not to use the Internet at all. Particularly if you are going to sites that you know you shouldn't be."

Talk with a parent about how and why you use the Internet.

Like Heather's parents, your parents may have heard scary stories about teens and children being exploited over the Internet. They may think that there is mostly bad stuff on the Internet, such as sites that feature pornography and violence. They may be afraid that a younger sibling may be looking over your shoulder while you are surfing these kinds of sites.

Your parents are not totally wrong. There are many inappropriate and even harmful sites on the Internet. By being honest with your parents about what you are doing on the Internet and the amount of time you spend on it, you can strike a balance that will satisfy both of you. Your parents might be concerned because they simply do not know very much about the Internet—and it is common to fear the unknown.

Go On-Line Together

Learning more about the Internet can be something that you and your parents do together. There are many books and Web sites for parents that address the topic of Internet safety for kids and teenagers. Some are listed in the Where to Go for Help section in this book.

Show these books and sites to your parents and encourage them to become informed about the Internet. You can talk together about what kinds of sites are okay for you to look at and what sites are not. Of course, your parents cannot protect you from everything—that's just part of growing up in the real world. But you can come to a reasonable agreement about staying safe on the Net. That is in your best interest too.

By showing your parents that you can use the Internet responsibly, you can put their minds at ease and earn their respect for your surfing time. If your parents are concerned that you are spending too much time on-line, talk with them about agreeing on a reasonable amount of time for you to spend per day or per week.

Software for Safety in Cyberspace

Your parents may want to purchase filtering or blocking software to protect you or younger siblings from accessing inappropriate material. Blocking software prevents access to a certain list of sites.

Sometimes the person who buys the software is able to put together his or her own list of "bad" sites. Other times, the software companies put the lists together themselves and do not allow the purchaser to add or remove sites from the list. One of the problems with blocking software is that there are way too many sites out there for reviewers (the people who decide whether or not a site is appropriate for young people) to keep track of. So any list of "bad" sites will be incomplete.

Filtering software blocks sites that use certain key-words. For example, your parents might choose to block any sites containing the word "sex." But the problem with filtering software is that it also blocks sites that contain the keywords but are not inappropriate or harmful. If the filtered keyword is "drug," sites that contain helpful anti-drug information will be blocked along with pro-drug sites. Like blocking software, some filtering programs come with the keywords already selected, while others allow the user to select which keywords to block.

Outgoing filtering is another kind of protection. With this software, certain information is blocked from being sent to others on-line, such as your name, address, or telephone number.

Your parents may want to install this kind of soft-ware to make sure that you or younger siblings do not accidentally give out personal information on-line. When a computer is running this software, if certain information is entered it shows up to the receiver simply as "xxxx."

Filtering software can block your access to certain sites.

Monitoring and tracking software allows parents to get information about how much time their kids have spent on-line and what sites they have visited. The parent can put a limit on the amount of time spent on-line; if the child tries to stay on longer, the software will prevent him or her from continuing to use the computer.

If your parents choose to use some kind of protective software, you may feel that it means that they do not trust you. Think of it instead as meaning that they want to protect you. If you have younger brothers or sisters who also go on-line, the software may be intended more for them than for you. You might just have to put up with it until they become older.

If you really think the software your parents use is

unfair—if it blocks genuinely informative and interesting sites rather than just inappropriate ones—talk to them about it. Maybe you can come to some sort of agreement. They might be willing to use your input to help them customize the software so it makes them feel as though you are protected without your feeling prevented from going to worthwhile sites.

Chapter 3

On Your Own in Cyberspace

Sanjay wanted to be a computer programmer someday. He loved nothing more than surfing the Web and adding new touches to his own site. When he started going out with Shauna, he put a picture of her on his site so that his friends and relatives in other cities could see what his new girlfriend looked like.

Sanjay was horrified when one day he got an e-mail from a stranger that said, "Your girlfriend is pretty cute. Does she go to Union High too? Maybe I'll have to check her out in person." Sanjay had put Shauna's first name under her picture, had mentioned on his site that he went to Union High School, and had given the name of his town. Was that enough information for someone to track down Shauna if he really wanted to? Sanjay suddenly wondered whether he had accidentally put his new girlfriend in danger.

Web Site Safety

The latest software makes designing your own Web site fun and fairly easy. Having your very own presence on the Internet is a great way to be creative and to express yourself.

But there is a flip side. Remember that anyone can stumble onto your Web site—perfect strangers can find out things about you and your life. Even if you only give your Web site address to friends and relatives, that is no guarantee that other people will not see it too. Keep this in mind when you are deciding how to present yourself on the Net.

Do not give out personal information such as your telephone number or address, and do not reveal personal details that you would not want a stranger to know. To be perfectly safe, do not reveal anything personal at all. Be equally careful about providing any information about friends or family members.

Be especially careful when posting photos. Never post a photo of someone else on your site without asking for that person's permission first. If you do post photographs, consider making them more private by requiring visitors to type in a password before being able to view the pictures.

Another thing to be careful of is the use of copyrighted material on your site. It may be tempting to include music from your favorite band, material from a book or magazine, or even material from other sites. But this material may be copyrighted, which means that it

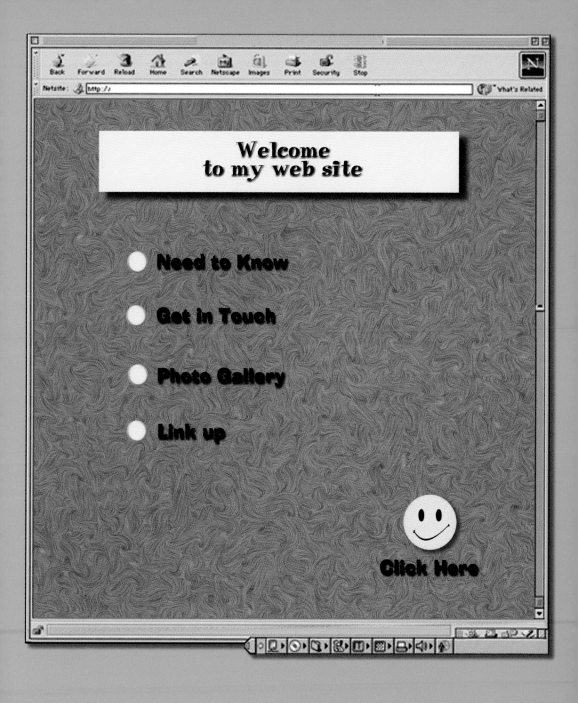

This is the home page of one teen's Web site.

is illegal to use it without the owner's permission. You can try to contact the Webmaster of a site that contains material you want to borrow, but keep in mind that the Webmaster may have borrowed the material from somewhere else and may not be in a position to grant you permission to use it. The Web site http://www.benedict.com provides further information on copyrighted material.

Copyrighted material can sometimes be used in a limited way called fair use. However, fair use guidelines for the Web are still under development.

E-Mail

E-mail was first used in the 1970s, but it did not really come into common use until the 1990s. Today, it is rapidly becoming one of the most popular forms of communication.

For the price of a telephone call—or less—you can send e-mail anywhere in the world. It is a great way to keep in touch with faraway friends and family. It has been estimated that 300 million e-mail messages cross the information superhighway every day. Within eight years, it is predicted that the number will grow to 5 billion.

E-mail is both fast and convenient. You and the person you are communicating with do not need to be online at the same time. You can write messages and read your e-mail at your own convenience. E-mail also gives you a lot of flexibility: You can delete messages without reading them, read mail without responding to it,

The following email interface is shown:

In

Who	Date	K	Subject

«No Recipient», 5:39 PM –0500, «No Subject»

BIN HEX ✓QP   Send

```
       To:  The Reader
     From:  Jane Doe <janed@yahoo.com>
  Subject:  Safety in Cyberspace
       Cc:
      Bcc:
X-Attachments:
```

Always remember to use cyberspace safely. :-)

E-mail is a great way to communicate with friends in faraway places.

or even send mail back to the sender unopened. "Smart" e-mail programs are being developed that can help you to manage your e-mail by sorting and prioritizing it before you even see it.

Because you cannot see or speak directly to the person you are e-mailing, and he or she cannot see or speak directly to you, e-mail may seem like an anonymous form of communication. You and an e-mail pal may not even know each other's real names.

This anonymity may make you feel that it is okay to write things to a person that you would not say to someone in "real life." But e-mail *is* real life. Remember that there is an actual person at the other end.

Because there are no visual cues—such as facial or

31

hand gestures—when using e-mail, it is easy for things said over e-mail to be misinterpreted. You cannot smile or chuckle to let someone know that a sarcastic comment is a joke. E-mail makes it easy to write a message quickly without really thinking about it, and you may write something that the recipient takes the wrong way. Try to proofread your e-mail before sending it to make sure it expresses exactly what you mean to say.

E-Mail Dangers and Annoyances

E-mail has developed its own vocabulary of terms. Unfortunately, many of these terms describe common abuses of e-mail. The Internet is changing so fast that new words come into the language all the time—too quickly to capture them all in a book—but here are a few of the most important ones right now:

"Flame wars" are when people send heckling, abusive, or offensive messages back and forth.

E-mail "bombs" are an overload of junk e-mail or hateful messages.

"Spamming," or sending out junk e-mail, is when a company or individual sends the same e-mail message to a large number of people at once. A man in Philadelphia became known as the "Spam King" for sending out up to twenty-five million promotional e-mails every day. Needless to say, this did not make him very popular. He was even sued for his actions. Recently, there has been talk of passing laws against spamming.

Anonymous re-mailer is an on-line service that hides

the sender's identity, allowing e-mail to be sent from a fake address. In 1997 hackers sent hundreds of e-mails to federal lawmakers warning that all of the files on U.S. Senate computers would be deleted. (A hacker is a person who gains illegal access to a computer system or network and sometimes tampers with its information.) Most of these e-mail messages were sent with fake return addresses.

"Finger servers" allow a person to find out any information that you gave when you signed up with an Internet Service Provider (ISP). All that the person needs to know is your full e-mail address; if they contact the ISP, they can obtain any other information about you that is on file. This may include your name, address, and telephone number.

You can also use a finger server to find out exactly what information about you is available on-line. When you enter your e-mail address in the finger server, you will be able to see what a stranger might be able to find out about you. If you discover that personal information about you is available and could be revealed, contact your ISP immediately to change or block the information.

A "computer virus" is a computer program hidden within another program. The virus produces copies of itself and inserts the copies into other programs, usually for the purpose of disrupting activity or destroying programs. You cannot get a computer virus just by reading e-mail or Web site material, but it is possible to get one by downloading material sent as an e-mail attachment.

In the spring of 1999, computer viruses caused a new scare for computer users. A virus—dubbed "Melissa" by its creator—created havoc for e-mail users around the world. Like most new computer viruses, Melissa arrived in an attachment to an unsolicited message via e-mail.

When an e-mail user opened the attachment, Melissa did its dirty work. In a matter of seconds, it sent duplicate messages and attachments that contained passwords and web addresses for pornography sites to the first fifty people in the e-mail address book of the initial receiver of the message. If any of *those* users opened the attachment, the process repeated itself.

And so Melissa replicated itself over and over again within the systems of hundreds of thousands of computer users around the world. In just a few days, Melissa was detected on computer systems across the United States as well as China and Germany. Systems used by members of the U.S. Congress were affected, as were some used by the U.S. Marines Corps.

Compared to earlier viruses, Melissa was not that deadly. For individual computer users, Melissa was more of an annoyance than a danger—a virus that caused one heck of a headache but did not threaten or destroy the user's files. Its chief purpose seems to have been simply to reproduce itself again and again.

Even so, experts in the computer industry quickly characterized Melissa as highly destructive. Chris Taylor, the cyberspace correspondent for *Time* magazine, described

Melissa as a "menace to wired society." Melissa was most damaging not to individual users but to computer servers, which are computers with large memory capacities used to provide services to other computers linked through a network. The sheer number of messages generated by Melissa overwhelmed such servers, interrupting all kinds of functions along the connected network. More than 300 networks had to be shut down for some time because of Melissa.

According to Steven White, a virus researcher at the IBM Corporation, "Melissa represents a new page in the history of viruses," because of the way it spread and the speed at which it spread. Although Melissa's creator was quickly caught—he now faces up to forty years in prison for violating laws prohibiting the "interruption of public communication"—the trouble the virus caused will take a long time to undo.

In the opinion of many experts, the greatest damage caused by Melissa is to the confidence of computer users communicating in cyberspace. As the Internet becomes increasingly important to the world's economy, any reduction in confidence about the safety of cyberspace has serious economic consequences.

So if Melissa does represent a whole new kind of virus, how can computer users protect themselves? For the most part, experts say, the best protection is the same old advice: Do not open e-mail attachments received from strangers. If a total stranger walked up to you on the street, handed you a package, and ran away, you wouldn't open the package—right? Practice the same kind of caution in cyberspace.

Make sure that your computer has been installed with anti-virus software to protect it from this danger and be cautious about downloading material sent as an attachment to an e-mail if you are unsure about the sender or the contents of the attachment. E-mail virus scanners are also available; contact your ISP provider for more information.

Finally, be aware of e-mail scams and hoaxes. You will probably encounter e-mail messages that warn about viruses or seem to be trying to raise money for a cause; these are usually scams. Do not be fooled by messages that describe what seems like an easy "get-rich-quick" scheme. If it sounds too good to be true, it probably is! Several sites provide information on avoiding scams. Check out http://www.scambusters.org and another site provided by the National Consumers League, http://www.fraud.org.

Chapter 4

Staying Safe on E-mail

There are other things to watch out for when you are using e-mail. Someone else can send an e-mail using your name and e-mail address. Be aware of this if you get an e-mail from someone you've never heard of before who acts as if he or she has already heard from you. Don't feel as though you should reply to someone simply because the person has succeeded in contacting you at your e-mail address! If a stranger called you at home, would you feel that you had to talk to him? Apply these same rules of basic safety to your e-mail correspondence. It is better to be considered rude than an easy target.

Hate speech transmitted over e-mail may involve threatening or offensive remarks about your race, religion, or ethnicity. This is not illegal, but it is worth reporting to the sender's ISP as an abuse of the

Report offensive and harassing e-mail messages to the sender's ISP.

e-mail service. (In 1997 the U.S. Supreme Court ruled that certain parts of the Telecommunications Act designed to protect minors from indecent speech were in conflict with the right to free speech guaranteed in the U.S. Constitution.)

If you do get a harassing or offensive e-mail, try to copy down everything that appears in the "header" section of the message. Give this information to the sender's ISP when you call with a complaint.

E-Mail and Privacy

E-mail may feel like a private, secure form of communication. You type in a password to access your e-mail, you send messages only to certain people, and you delete messages after you have read them. But e-mail is not really private.

To maintain your privacy over e-mail, pick an e-mail address and user name that does not reveal your real name or any other personal information about yourself. If you are female, you may want to pick a gender-neutral user name so that your gender is concealed when you are in a chat room or newsgroup. Internet stalkers are more likely to target a user with a name that sounds like it belongs to a woman.

If you use e-mail through your school's server, you may have even less privacy. Legally, e-mail sent from a school district's server is the property of the school district. Likewise, e-mail sent from an employer's server belongs to that employer, and so they have the legal right to access it. Employees have been fired for e-mail messages that they have written. At some companies it is forbidden to use company e-mail for any personal communications.

In any case, a student's e-mail should not be examined without good reason, just as a student's locker cannot be searched by school officials without just cause. If you have Internet access at school, part of your school's AUP should specify the circumstances under which that privacy can be violated.

What Can You Do?

You may feel helpless if you are being harassed over e-mail. After all, if you do not even know the person's

In *The Net,* Sandra Bullock's character finds that her identity has been stolen by a cyberstalker.

real name, what can you do? One option is to contact the abuse department of the sender's ISP, give the person's e-mail address, and complain that the person has been harassing you. The ISP can cancel the person's e-mail account. But keep in mind that the ISP may not respond to your complaint immediately. Most ISPs get more complaints than they can handle right away.

Even if you succeed in getting the ISP to cancel the harasser's account, the person can just get another ISP and e-mail account and start sending you messages again. If this happens, you might want to consider changing your own ISP and e-mail address.

You can also contact your ISP and find out how to block messages from a particular individual. Many popular e-mail packages feature tools to filter and sort e-mail.

If the sender's messages to you are threatening or disturbing, report this "cyberstalking" to the police. Be aware, however, that this type of harassment is a new thing for most police departments and they are still trying to figure out how to deal with it. Cyberstalking is so new that many states that have existing anti-stalking laws have not extended the legislation to cover cyberstalking.

Cyberstalking laws do exist in seven states—Alaska, Arizona, Connecticut, Michigan, New York, Oklahoma, and Wyoming. More states will probably institute such laws in the future as the problem becomes more wide-spread. The Telecommunications Act of 1996 also offers some protection against cyberstalking.

Netiquette

Mimi and her friends loved exchanging the jokes they received over e-mail. As soon as Mimi got a joke from a friend, she would forward it to everyone on her long e-mail list of classmates and friends. What she didn't realize was that she had typed in one of the addresses wrong, and she had actually been sending jokes to the address of a stranger. One day, she got an angry e-mail message from the stranger in which he complained about all the joke e-mails. "I'm sick of all of your stupid jokes," he wrote. "If you don't stop sending them to me, I'll report you and get your e-mail taken away."

The Internet is developing its own code of etiquette—
sometimes called "netiquette"— or proper and polite
way of behaving. You can practice netiquette by not
clogging others' mailboxes with unnecessary messages.
Most people do not appreciate "chain letters" sent over
e-mail, for example, especially when the letters pressure
the receiver to continue the chain. Think before forwarding a joke to everyone on your address list: Is it
really that funny? Will everyone appreciate it? Do you
think that everyone on your list really wants to see it?

When sending e-mail, always double-check to be sure
that you are sending it to the correct address. When
sending e-mail to a group list, check that *all* of the
addresses are correct, and always take a person's
address off the group list immediately if they request
that you do so.

One very convenient feature of e-mail is that messages can easily be forwarded from one person to
another. But be careful about forwarding. When you forward a message, you also pass along a person's e-mail
address (and whatever personal information might be
contained in the message) without that person's knowl-
edge. Check with the person whose e-mail you want to
forward to make sure that it is okay with him or her.
For the same reason, do not send personal information
in your own messages unless you really trust the person at the other end and can be sure he or she will not
pass it on to someone else.

Using e-mail messages to sell things is considered a

violation of e-mail etiquette. Many of the major ISPs have guidelines that restrict the posting or sending of advertising or promotional materials except in areas that have been set aside just for that purpose. If you send a message that is actually an advertisement, someone who receives that message may report you to your ISP and your account could be canceled. You can also report people who send you advertising messages.

If you send an attachment to an e-mail message, check back to make sure the person you sent it to was able to read it. Many e-mail systems have problems dealing with attachments. Before sending a very large attachment, ask first to find out whether the person at the other end will be able to receive it. If he or she has a very slow modem, it may take a long time to view your attachment.

Chapter 5

Chat Rooms and News Groups

*K*arim was excited when he discovered a chat room just for fans of his favorite band. He liked to see what other fans thought of its new songs and videos, and to discuss upcoming concerts. He exchanged a lot of messages with someone who also spent a lot of time in the chat room whose e-mail nickname was Charlie.

One day Karim typed a message in which he complained that his parents would not allow him to go to the band's upcoming concert because it was in another city that was two hours away. "Wow, that's crazy," Charlie e-mailed back. "Your parents must be really strict. Listen, I've got an extra ticket to that show, so why don't you come along? Tell your parents you're staying over at a friend's house. I'll pick you up and drop you off, and they'll never know the difference."

Karim knew that it was not a good idea to meet up

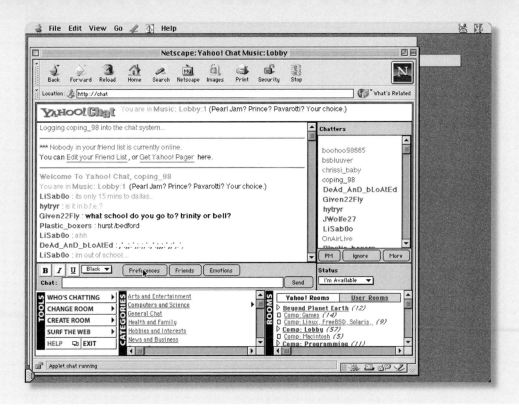

Chat rooms can be fun, but be aware of safety precautions.

with someone he had met on-line without letting his parents know. But he was also tempted. Charlie was right—his parents were being unreasonable about this. And he and Charlie had so much in common that Charlie had to be a normal guy, Karim thought.

Chat Rooms

Chat rooms are places on the Internet where you can have a live "conversation" with others who are on-line at the same time. Everything you type can be seen by others who are in the chat room.

There are different kinds of chat rooms. Some are designed just for people with a particular background or interest. For example, there might be a chat room just for single parents or one for people interested in *Star Trek* movies.

Not all chat rooms are focused on fun or harmless topics, however. You may stumble onto a chat room organized around a topic like cults, sex, or violence. It is best to avoid chat rooms like these. Even if you do not take the topic very seriously, others in the chat room might. They may want to do some of the activities that they write about and may want to get you involved as well.

Sometimes chat rooms have someone who leads discussions. Others are more open. Some chat rooms even have a monitor who can ask someone to leave the chat room if the person is not behaving in an appropriate manner.

Some chat rooms are organized for teens to meet each other or to discuss topics of interest to teens. But chat rooms that appeal to teenagers may also appeal to stalkers or pedophiles who are trying to find young victims. Be aware that the person you are "talking" to may not be who he or she claims to be. A person in a chat room may pretend to be someone else just so that he or she can strike up a conversation with you. Even in what is supposed to be a "teens only" chat room, there is no way to tell if a person who says she is a 16-year-old student is actually a 45-year-old man!

Be careful about going into "private" chat rooms if someone asks you to do so. Think about why the other person does not want others in the chat room to read

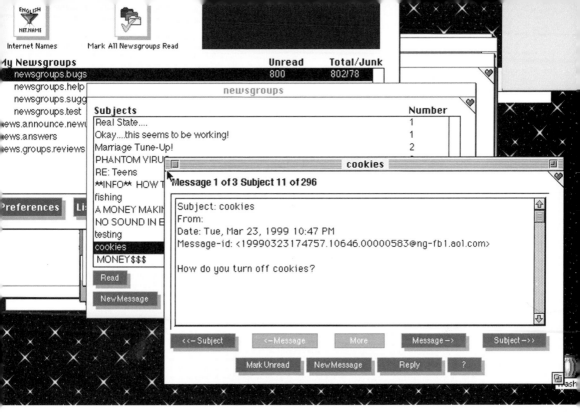

My Newsgroups   Unread   Total/Junk
newsgroups.bugs   800   802/78
newsgroups.help
newsgroups.sugg
newsgroups.test
news.announce.new
news.answers
news.groups.reviews

newsgroups

Subjects	Number
Real State....	1
Okay....this seems to be working!	1
Marriage Tune-Up!	2
PHANTOM VIRU	
RE: Teens	
INFO HOW T	
fishing	
A MONEY MAKI	
NO SOUND IN E	
testing	
cookies	
MONEY$$$	

Read

NewMessage

Preferences   Li

cookies

Message 1 of 3 Subject 11 of 296

Subject: cookies
From:
Date: Tue, Mar 23, 1999 10:47 PM
Message-id: <19990323174757.10646.00000583@ng-fb1.aol.com>

How do you turn off cookies?

<<– Subject   <–Message   More   Message –>   Subject –>>

Mark Unread   NewMessage   Reply   ?

Trash

Chat rooms and news groups allow people who share an interest to discuss that particular topic.

what he or she is writing to you. First, find out what the other person wants to talk about. He or she may just want to talk in more detail about something related to the chat room topic. But don't ever feel trapped into talking to someone more than you'd like or that it would be rude to ignore a message if it makes you feel uncomfortable.

You and some friends might enjoy talking in a so-called private chat room. But these rooms may be listed in a directory, and there may be no way to prevent others from entering the conversation.

Adults in chat rooms may also try to befriend younger people by offering advice and being supportive. Sometimes this is harmless and can even be helpful—but be aware that it may also be a way to try to get you to lower your guard. Do not start telling your personal problems to someone in a chat room just because the person seems to be understanding. Be especially alert if the other person is very critical of your parents, friends, or teachers. He may be trying to turn you against your support network and to get you to listen only to him.

Be especially careful to not give out your real name, address, or other personal information in a chat room.

News Groups

News groups are also called bulletin boards or forums. Like chat rooms, they are often organized around particular subjects. They are places to share information and to ask and answer questions on a certain topic.

For example, if you want to know what other fans of a particular band think of the band's latest album, you might post a message on the news group dedicated to that band. Users in a news group about Mexican cooking might exchange recipes. Users in a news group on depression might share information about new treatments and therapies. Files containing things like computer programs or illustrations can also be posted in news groups.

News groups are different from chat rooms in that communications within them do not take place in "real time," which means the message you post is not seen immediately by other people. But this does not necessarily make them safer.

Make sure a parent checks out any on-line friend that you would like to meet in person.

Usually, anyone in the news group can read something you have typed, even if your response is just to one other person. When you post something in a news group you reveal your e-mail address, which puts you at risk for receiving anything from harassing messages to simply bothersome junk mail. As with chat rooms, be careful about revealing anything personal about yourself. This information could be used in the wrong way by someone wanting to harass or victimize you.

Some of the material posted in news groups may be offensive or even illegal (such as sexually explicit pictures of children). Talk to your parents or a trusted adult about material you find disturbing. You may even want to report obscene material to your ISP.

If you are in a chat room or news group and you receive a threatening message, or any kind of message that makes you feel uncomfortable, do not respond. Responding is what the sender wants you to do. The sender is just trying to get your attention and get you to communicate with him or her. If the messages continue, you might want to stop visiting the chat room or news group.

"Meeting" Someone On-Line

Using the Internet and e-mail can expose you to lots of new people. This can be exciting, but it may also be dangerous. You have already read about how important it is to keep your identity private when you are on-line. There have been terrible cases of innocent people being victimized by someone they agreed to meet after first meeting on-line.

Of course, not everyone using the Internet or e-mail is a dangerous person. There are plenty of normal adults and teens just like you who go on-line for fun and information.

In the course of your travels on-line, you may meet someone who seems to share a lot of your interests. You may develop a regular correspondence with that person and feel close to him or her even though you have never actually met. You and the other person may want to talk on the telephone. But be sure to check with your parents before giving out your telephone number or before calling someone else's number that you got on-line.

If you and your new friend want to meet in person after speaking on the telephone, talk to your parents about whether they are comfortable with that. If possible, your parents should speak with the other person's parents to arrange the meeting. And, of course, your parents should go with you to the first meeting.

This may seem overly cautious to you. But remember that someone you meet on-line is still a total stranger—you simply cannot tell very much about what a person is really like from how he or she behaves on-line. And people who use the Internet for criminal purposes are very good—and very experienced—at manipulating other people by telling them what they want to hear.

Chapter 6

Staying Balanced

*J*oey had always been a pretty shy kid. At the time he started junior high school his best friend moved away. Joey had trouble making new friends. He spent a lot of afternoons surfing the Net.

His mom urged him to do things outside of the house—like playing basketball at the neighborhood court or joining a club or sports team at school. But Joey did not really feel like making the effort. It was much easier to come home from school and turn on the computer.

Once he got on-line, a whole new world opened up for him. He would visit his favorite sites and play computer games. It was not long before he was more comfortable communicating with total strangers in chat rooms than talking with real classmates and peers.

Joey did not really see anything wrong with his Internet habit. But when he finished junior high and

Spending all of your time on the Net can make it difficult to maintain friendships.

entered high school, he realized that he did not really know any of his classmates. When his mom insisted that he try out for the soccer team, he did—but the coach did not pick him. It made Joey wish that he had kept playing soccer during junior high instead of spending so much time on his computer. He tried to be more sociable, but it was difficult for him. He had forgotten how much harder it was to meet new people in person rather than on-line.

As we said, the Internet is a terrific invention. In the next few years it will no doubt be possible to do even more things with the Internet. Most jobs today involve being able to use a computer, so it is also important to learn these skills. That's part of the reason why so many schools now have computers and Internet connections.

But as with other activities, sometimes there can be too much of a good thing. You may enjoy surfing the Web and reading and writing e-mail. You may feel like you could stay on the computer for hours. But don't forget about other important things that only happen off-line— like spending time with your family and friends, exercising, helping out around the house, and participating in sports and other school activities.

It is important to have other hobbies besides the Internet. Do not neglect your off-line social life just because you have so many people to exchange e-mail messages with. There is still nothing like face-to-face

Real time spent with friends is important and cannot be replaced.

contact and spending real time with friends, even if it is just hanging out at your house or going to a movie.

Having a lively social life over e-mail is not a replacement for the real thing. Imagine if one day you could not get on-line. Who would you call? What would you do? If you have trouble thinking of alternatives to being on-line, you're probably spending too much time on the computer.

And of course, spending time on the Internet should never take time away from one of your most important responsibilities—homework. You can learn a lot from surfing the Net. Sometimes it may even help you with your homework by helping you to find answers to research questions or by giving you information about

Don't neglect your studies just to surf the Internet.

a topic. But the computer cannot do your homework for you. School is your job while you are a teenager—that's where most of your time should be spent. As educational as the Internet can be, it is easy to spend a lot of time exploring other things on-line too. Without even realizing it you can spend two hours on-line—with nothing to show for it.

It is important to be objective about the Internet. It certainly is an amazing way to exchange information and connect with people, but at the end of the day it is still real people who make the Internet what it is—and real people make mistakes and do things that are not smart or safe.

Remember that what you read on a Web site is not necessarily the whole truth—or true at all. It may just be someone's opinion, or what a person would like you to believe. The motives for telling you such things may not be immediately apparent. This may especially be the case when people are talking about themselves— they may not be telling you the whole story.

By playing it safe in cyberspace, you can take advantage of everything this exciting new world of communication has to offer while steering clear of danger. As cyberspace gets more complicated and more crowded, it is important to know how to protect yourself.

Glossary

blocking software Software that can be programmed to keep the user from accessing certain Web sites.

chat room A place on the Internet where participants can exchange messages with others who are also on-line.

cyberspace The world of the Internet that includes Web sites, chat rooms, and other places to communicate and get information.

e-mail An extremely popular form of communication in which messages are sent from one computer to another.

filtering software Software that can be programmed to screen out certain kinds of Web sites.

flaming Sending e-mail messages with a very critical tone, often to someone who has violated netiquette.

HTML Abbreviation for hypertext mark-up language, which is the computer code used to create Web sites.

hypertext See HTML.

Internet A worldwide network of computers.

Internet Service Provider (ISP) A company or institution that provides access to the Inernet, often for a fee.

modem A device that uses a telephone line to connect a computer to the Internet.

netiquette A code of behavior for users of the Internet.

spamming Sending "junk" e-mail messages to many people at once.

World Wide Web A network of hypertext links or hyperlinks that allow Internet users to move easily from one Web site to another.

Where to Go for Help

Copyright Web Site
http://www.benedict.com
Provides information on using copyrighted material.

CyberAngels
http://cyberangels.org/
Volunteer organization that "patrols" cyberspace, reviewing Web sites for content that is appropriate for families and children.

Homework Heaven
http://www.homeworkheaven.com
Provides useful educational information.

Internet Public Library
Youth Division
http://www.ipl.org/youth/

National Center for Missing and Exploited Children CyberTipline
http://www.missingkids.org
(800) 843-5678

National Consumers League
http://www.fraud.org

Netiquette Guide
http://www.fau.edu/rinadli/net/index.htm

New York Public Library Teen Link
http://www.nypl.org/branch/teen/teenlink.html
Check this site for lots of links just for teens, including links to sites that will help you with homework-related problems and questions.

World Kids Network
http://www.worldkids.net
Visit this site for "Safe Surf Guides."

For Further Reading

Ahmad, Nyla. *Cybersurfer: The Owl Internet Guide for Kids.* New York: Owl Books, 1996.

Bruno, Bonnie. *Internet Family Fun: A Parents' Guide to Safe Surfing.* San Francisco: No Starch Press, 1997.

Burgstahler, Sheryl. *New Kids on the Net: A Tutorial for Teachers, Parents, and Students.* Boston: Allyn & Bacon, 1997.

Gelman, Robert, Stanton McCandlish, and Ester Dyson. *Protecting Yourself Online: The Definitive Resource on Safety, Freedom, and Privacy in Cyberspace.* New York: HarperCollins, 1998.

Gralla, Preston. *Online Kids: A Young Surfer's Guide to Cyberspace.* New York: Wiley, 1996.

Levine, John R., Carol Baroudi, and Margaret Levine Young. *The Internet for Dummies,* 5th ed. IDG Books Worldwide, 1998.

McCormick, Anita Louise. *The Internet: Surfing the Issues.* Springfield, NJ: Enslow, 1998.

Young, Kimberly S. *Caught in the Net: How to Recognize the Signs of Internet Addiction and a Winning Strategy for Recovery.* New York: Wiley, 1998.

Index

About the Author

Jennifer Croft is a freelance writer in Massachusetts who has written several books for young adults.

Photo Credits

Cover photo by Thaddeus Harden. P. 10 © *NY Post*-Don Halasy (*New York Post*)/Corbis; p. 40 © Joyce Rudolph/Everett Collection; all other photos by Thaddeus Harden.